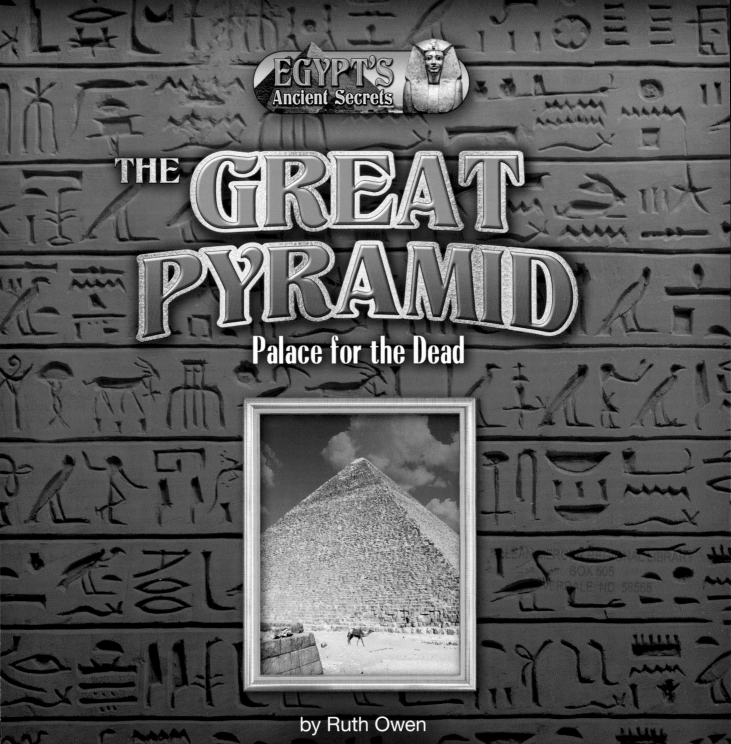

EGYPT'S Ancient Secrets

THE GREAT PYRAMID

Palace for the Dead

by Ruth Owen

Consultant: Dr. Angela McDonald
Subject Specialist and University Teacher—Archaeology, Classics, and Egyptology
Centre for Open Studies, University of Glasgow, Scotland, UK

BEARPORT
PUBLISHING

New York, New York

Credits

Cover and Title Page, © Danita Delimont/Shutterstock, © Pius Lee/Shutterstock, and © Nemeziya/Shutterstock; 4–5, © Sol90Images; 6–7, © Dan Breckwoldt/Shutterstock; 8, © Dorling Kindersley/Getty Images; 9T, © De Agostini/Getty Images; 9B, © Murat Hajdarhodzic/Shutterstock; 10L, © mangojuicy/Shutterstock; 10R, Public Domain; 11, © Dudarev Mikhail/Shutterstock; 11TL, © De Agostini/Getty Images; 11TR, © De Agostini/Getty Images; 12–13, Jose Antonio Penas/Science Photo Library; 14, © Jose Lucas/Alamy; 15, © Sol90Images; 16, © Danita Delimont/Alamy; 17T, © Sebastian Grant/Shutterstock; 17B, © Peter Horree/Alamy; 18, © Reuters/Alamy; 19, © Kenneth Garrett/Getty Images; 20, Public Domain; 21T, © Ruby Tuesday Books; 21B, © Baloncici/Istock Photo; 22T, © Arco Images GmbH/Alamy; 22B, © Pius Lee/Shutterstock; 23L, © De Agostini/Getty Images; 23R, © De Agostini/Getty Images; 24, © Kenneth Garrett/Getty Images; 25, © Patrick Chapuis/Getty Images; 26, © Kokhanchikov/Shutterstock; 27, © Patryk Kosmider/Shutterstock; 28, © Patrick Chapuis/Gamma-Rapho/Getty Images; 29, Public Domain; 31, © Dudarev Mikhail/Shutterstock.

Publisher: Kenn Goin
Editor: Jessica Rudolph
Creative Director: Spencer Brinker
Photo Researcher: Ruby Tuesday Books Ltd

Library of Congress Cataloging-in-Publication Data

Names: Owen, Ruth, 1967- author.
Title: The Great Pyramid : palace for the dead / by Ruth Owen.
Other titles: Egypt's ancient secrets.
Description: New York, New York : Bearport Publishing, 2017. | Series:
   Egypt's ancient secrets | Includes bibliographical references and index.
Identifiers: LCCN 2016054069 | ISBN 9781684020232 (library)
Subjects: LCSH: Great Pyramid (Egypt)—Juvenile literature.
Classification: LCC DT63 .O94 2017 | DDC 932—dc23
LC record available at https://lccn.loc.gov/2016054069

For more information, write to Bearport Publishing Company, Inc., 45 West 21st Street, Suite 3B, New York, New York 10010.
Printed in the United States of America.

10 9 8 7 6 5 4 3 2 1

Contents

Built for Eternity

The year is 2570 B.C. It's early morning on a rocky desert plain in Egypt. As the sun rises, thousands of workers hurry toward a giant, half-completed **pyramid** that looms in the sky like a mountain. Soon, teams of men are pulling on ropes to haul huge blocks of stone toward the pyramid. The men are **chanting** as they work.

Pyramid

Block of stone

4

Other workers can be seen high on the pyramid's sloping sides. Against the huge structure, they look like tiny ants. These men are the skilled **stonemasons** who precisely guide each giant block of stone into position. Under the hot desert sun, the grueling construction work will continue hour after hour until sunset.

One day, years from now, the enormous structure will finally be finished. Then the Great Pyramid will tower over the desert for all eternity.

Experts think it took workers up to 20 years to build the Great Pyramid— from around the years 2580 to 2560 B.C.

A Giant Pyramid

The Great Pyramid of Giza is one of the largest human-made structures on earth. Built from about 2.3 million blocks of limestone, the pyramid's base covers an area the size of ten football fields! When the pyramid was first built, it stood 481 feet (147 m) tall—the height of a 40-story building. At some time in its past, however, the tip of the pyramid was removed. Now it's 455 feet (139 m) tall.

The Great Pyramid is on the west bank of the Nile River, in the city of Giza. It stands across the river from Egypt's capital city of Cairo.

Mediterranean Sea

Great Pyramid of Giza — Cairo

EGYPT

Nile River

Red Sea

N W E S

Arctic Ocean

NORTH AMERICA

EUROPE

Atlantic Ocean

AFRICA

Pacific Ocean

Pacific Ocean

SOUTH AMERICA

Indian Ocean

AUSTRALIA

N W E S

Southern Ocean

ANTARCTICA

Today, around 4,500 years after it was built, the Great Pyramid is battered by time, but it still stands. So how were the ancient Egyptians able to build this huge structure without the use of high-tech tools—and what was its purpose?

The Great Pyramid is gigantic. Each of its four sides is 756 feet (230 m) long—the length of two football fields. Some of the blocks of stone that were used to build the pyramid weigh 1 ton (0.9 metric ton). Others weigh up to 50 tons (45 metric tons)—as much as a truck!

The Great Pyramid's four sides perfectly face north, east, south, and west. **Egyptologists** think that ancient **astronomers** used the stars to pinpoint the four directions and position the pyramid.

7

A Tomb for a King

The ancient Egyptians were skillful builders who created palaces, **temples**, and other buildings. Some of the most complex structures were tombs. These were graves, rooms, or buildings in which dead bodies were placed.

In ancient Egypt, people believed that after death, their **spirits** lived on in the **afterlife**. In order for this to happen, however, a person needed his or her body. The dead body was **preserved** as a mummy by **embalmers**. Then it was placed in a tomb, where it would be safe for all time.

This embalmer wears an Anubis mask. Anubis was the god of embalming.

Mummy

Embalmers dried out a dead body with salt, rubbed it with oils and animal fat, and then wrapped the body in bandages to create a mummy.

The Great Pyramid was built as the final resting place of the ancient Egyptian king **Pharaoh** Khufu. Like all pharaohs, as soon as he came to power, Khufu ordered the building of his tomb. No pharaoh had ever built such a large or complicated tomb before, though!

This statue is the only surviving image of Pharaoh Khufu.

Khufu wasn't the first pharaoh to build a pyramid-shaped tomb. More than 100 years before Khufu, a king named Pharaoh Djoser (JOH-serr) built a step pyramid with six levels. Over the centuries, the ancient Egyptians built more than 100 pyramids.

Construction Begins

Before work on his pyramid could begin, Pharaoh Khufu appointed a **vizier**. This powerful official would oversee the design and construction of the king's tomb.

Once a site for the pyramid was chosen, thousands of workers began gathering construction materials from around Khufu's kingdom. Close to the pyramid site, stonemasons dug a **quarry** into the ground. Here, they cut limestone blocks for the pyramid. By the time the pyramid was finished, the limestone quarry was 100 feet (30.5 m) deep and almost a mile (1.6 km) wide.

A modern-day limestone quarry

This is a statue of a man named Hemiunu, who was Khufu's vizier.

Granite would be used in parts of the inside of the pyramid. This rock was brought in from a different quarry hundreds of miles away. Large ships called barges, with crews of 500 sailors, sailed up the Nile River. These boats carried the giant slabs of the rock to the construction site.

To make tools, workers heated and melted copper over scorching-hot fires. Then the metal was shaped to make chisels for cutting the stone blocks. Tons of wood from far away had to be gathered as fuel for the fires.

This carving shows sailors carrying a large stone block on a barge.

Stone block

Ancient Egyptian copper chisel

Khufu chose to build his pyramid in the desert west of the Nile. The ancient Egyptians thought of this area as a place of death because the sun set, or died, in the west each night.

Moving the Stones

After stonemasons cut the blocks, a team of workers dragged each giant stone to the pyramid with ropes. Then, experts believe, the stone blocks may have been hauled up ramps that spiraled around the growing structure. Finally, the blocks were carefully pushed into position. Soon, the pyramid started to take shape.

The blocks may have been pulled along on wooden sledges. To help the sledges slide, workers likely poured water or milk on the sand to make it wet and slippery.

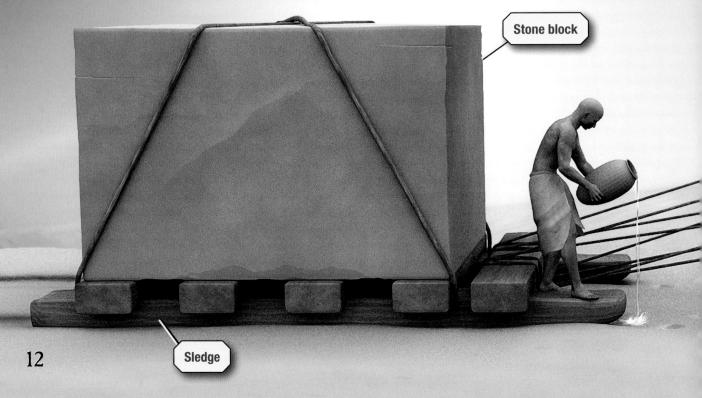

Stone block

Sledge

Once the pyramid was built, the rough blocks that are visible today were covered with a layer of highly polished white stones. Egyptologists believe that up to 30,000 people doing many different jobs worked on the Great Pyramid. To complete it in about 20 years, the builders must have worked ten-hour days and put one block in place every two minutes!

Ramp

The ramps were probably made of mud and small bits of stone.

The teams of pyramid builders had names such as *Endurance*, *Perfection*, and *Friends of Khufu*. The teams may have competed against each other, giving them a reason to work faster!

Inside the Pyramid

As the workers built the pyramid, they created passageways and chambers deep inside. They even dug a long tunnel into the rock beneath the pyramid. At the end of the tunnel, more than 200 feet (61 m) below ground, they carved a room. What was this dark, cavelike chamber to be used for? No one knows. Mysteriously, the underground chamber was never completed.

One room the builders did finish is the burial chamber for the pharaoh, called the King's Chamber. The walls and high ceiling of this large room were formed from about 60 enormous granite blocks. Inside the burial chamber, workers placed a **sarcophagus**. This large stone coffin would hold the body of their pharaoh.

The stone blocks were joined together using a mixture made of water and a rocky powder called gypsum. Once it dried, the mixture hardened.

The white, outside stones were so closely fitted together that it was not possible to slide a knife between them.

Layers of blocks fill the inside of the pyramid.

The sarcophagus is too big to fit through the passageway that leads to the king's burial chamber. This tells Egyptologists that the pyramid builders must have put the stone coffin in place and then built around it.

Khufu's sarcophagus

Narrow tunnels, or shafts

King's Chamber: Some of the granite blocks inside the burial chamber weigh 50 tons (45 metric tons).

Grand Gallery: This long, narrow corridor is 28 feet (8.5 m) high. It climbs steeply toward the King's Chamber.

Passageways

Underground tunnel

Queen's Chamber: In the 800s, pyramid explorers named this chamber, but it was never actually used as a burial place for any of Khufu's queens.

Underground chamber

15

The Builders' City

For many years, some Egyptologists thought the pyramid builders were slaves who were forced to work for the pharaoh. Today, experts have found **evidence** that shows this was not the case.

Close to the Great Pyramid, buried under layers of sand, **archaeologists** dug up a lost city! They found small, mud-brick houses and larger buildings, too. They believe the city was specially built for the pyramid builders.

Ruins of the city walls

An archaeologist examines pottery from the pyramid builders' city.

Egyptologists think that some workers, like the skilled stonemasons, worked on the pyramid all year long. Other, less skilled workers may have come to the site for just a few months out of the year.

The archaeologists found old bakeries that could have produced enough bread for thousands of people. They also dug up large quantities of bones from fish, sheep, goats, and cattle. Together, all this evidence showed that the pyramid builders were not poorly treated slaves. In fact, the workers had well-built homes and a good diet of bread, fish, and meat.

A sheep's skull

Living and Dying

Close to the pyramid builders' city, archaeologists have also found an ancient **cemetery**. After studying skeletons from the cemetery, scientists believe this is the place where workers were buried after they died. The bones show that the people had done hard **manual** work, such as hauling heavy stones. However, it was also clear to the scientists that the workers received medical care.

The pyramid builders were not buried in **elaborate** tombs. Their bodies were wrapped in linen bandages and laid in simple graves. A worker might have been buried with items he would have needed in the afterlife, such as a jar of beer and a knife for cutting meat.

The grave of a pyramid builder

The scientists examined one body with an **amputated** arm, and another skeleton with a missing leg. Both workers were probably injured while building the pyramid. The men had received help from a doctor, however, and had both lived for many years after their accidents.

Without doubt, the lives of the pyramid builders were difficult. Yet, most experts think the workers were probably proud to have worked on this important project for their pharaoh.

A stone sarcophagus containing the skeleton of an overseer

In the cemetery, archaeologists found a few small but elaborate tombs. These are the burial places of the overseers who managed the pyramid builders.

Khufu's Last Journey

After many years of construction, the Great Pyramid was ready to receive the king. There is no record of what happened after Pharaoh Khufu died. Egyptologists believe, however, that the king's mummy was probably laid in a wooden coffin. Then priests and **mourners** carried the coffin into the pyramid, up the Grand Gallery, and into the king's burial chamber.

These paintings from a tomb show a funeral (above) and mourners (right).

Inside the burial chamber, the coffin was laid in the sarcophagus. Then the priests placed beautiful furniture, jewels, and other objects inside the room for Khufu to use in the afterlife.

In ancient Egypt, thieves would try to break into tombs to steal the goods inside. To protect the pharaoh and his treasures from tomb robbers, the burial chamber was sealed off by three giant slabs of stone. Afterward, the priests and mourners left the pyramid. Then the entrance was sealed up with stone blocks—forever!

Burial chamber

Passageway

Slabs of stone were lowered into place.

The pyramid builders installed three slabs of stone in the ceiling of the passageway that led to the burial chamber. The stones were held in place by ropes. Once Khufu was inside the chamber, the stones were lowered.

When the pyramid's entrance was covered with stone blocks, it was impossible to see it from the outside. Today, the entrance has been uncovered.

Entrance

The Missing Mummy

In the years after Pharaoh Khufu's death, other pyramids, temples, and tombs were built at Giza. About 3,400 years passed by. Then, in the year 820, a group of Arab treasure hunters led by **Caliph** Al-Ma'mun broke into the Great Pyramid. The explorers could not find the pyramid's hidden entrance, so they cut a hole into one of its slopes. Over many months, they tunneled through the stone blocks.

Khufu's pyramid

Khafre's pyramid

Menkaure's pyramid

Alongside Khufu's pyramid, three small pyramids were built for his wives. Khufu's son, Pharaoh Khafre (KAF-ray), and his grandson, Pharaoh Menkaure (MEN-kow-ray), also built their pyramids at Giza. A giant statue called the Great Sphinx was carved there, too.

The Great Sphinx

Eventually, the men discovered the burial chamber. When the explorers broke into the King's Chamber, however, they found nothing but the empty stone sarcophagus. There was no treasure and no sign of Pharaoh Khufu's mummy!

Had ancient tomb robbers already found a way into the pyramid and stolen Khufu's treasure and his mummy? Or is there a more **intriguing** answer to this mystery?

These pictures show what it might have looked like as Al-Ma'mun's men explored the Grand Gallery (left) and King's Chamber (below).

The Mysterious Shafts

In modern times, Egyptologists have carefully explored the pyramid's passageways and chambers. However, they have yet to find any sign of Khufu's mummy.

As part of their investigations, Egyptologists studied two long, narrow shafts, or tunnels, that lead from the empty Queen's Chamber. The tunnels are just 8 inches (20 cm) wide—much too small for a person to crawl through. So scientists decided to use robots!

Robot

Shaft in Queen's Chamber

The giant slabs of stone that once protected the entrance to Khufu's burial chamber are gone. They were probably removed by pyramid explorers in the 1800s, who often used explosives to blast their way into passageways and chambers.

Several small robots have been used to explore the long shafts. Scientists discovered that each shaft is blocked at the end by a stone door. Each of the tiny stone doors contains two small pieces of metal—the only metal ever found within the Great Pyramid. What are the metal pieces for? So far, no one knows.

To see beyond one of these doors, a robot drilled a hole through it. On the other side, the robot discovered a tiny chamber with nothing inside. Beyond this, there was yet another small stone door.

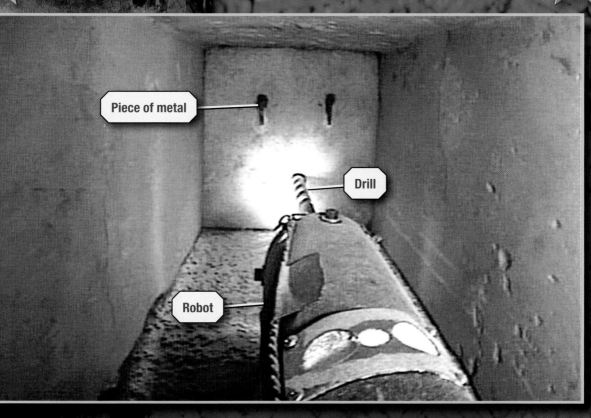

Piece of metal

Drill

Robot

The robot was fitted with cameras that filmed and photographed the shaft. On a computer screen, the robot's human operators could see exactly what it was doing.

A Secret Chamber?

What lies beyond the second door? Some experts believe that the long, narrow shaft simply comes to an end. They also have a **theory** that both shafts are **symbolic**. They may be magical passageways through which ancient Egyptians believed Pharaoh Khufu's spirit would have traveled into the afterlife.

The sun god, Ra, sailed across the sky on a barge, or barque.

According to one theory, once Khufu entered the afterlife, he would sail through the skies with the sun god, Ra.

Other experts disagree. They think that the shafts could perhaps be a clue to the mystery of Khufu's missing mummy. Is there an undiscovered burial chamber hidden deep within the pyramid? Do the shafts wind and climb through the pyramid's stonework, perhaps leading to this chamber?

Only time and more investigations will tell. For now, only the Great Pyramid knows the answer to the mystery.

If the shafts were created as passageways for the king's spirit, why do they lead from the Queen's Chamber? Some experts believe this room may have been built to hold a small statue of Khufu, not the queens' mummies. The statue would have been a symbol of the king's spirit.

Egypt's Ancient Secrets

Experts have uncovered some of the Great Pyramid's secrets, but many mysteries still remain.

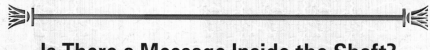

Are There Hidden Passageways and Chambers Inside the Great Pyramid?

Over the years, archaeologists have investigated the inside of the pyramid and discovered chambers and passages. Only a tiny part of the interior has been explored, however. Could there be more secret tunnels and rooms to be found?

An archaeologist exploring a passageway inside the pyramid

Is There a Message Inside the Shaft?

In 2011, a robot named Djedi examined one of the shafts that leads from the Queen's Chamber. Djedi inserted a tiny camera on a long, flexible stem into the chamber beyond the first door. The robot took photos that show 4,500-year-old **hieroglyphs** on the walls of the tiny chamber. Egyptologists are now studying these letters and symbols to discover what they say. Could they explain the reason for the shafts?

What Was the Purpose of the King's Chamber?

If Khufu was never actually buried in the King's Chamber, why was this room built? Some experts think the burial chamber and stone sarcophagus could be an ancient trick played by the pyramid builders. If tomb robbers found the room and sarcophagus empty, they might think the pharaoh's treasures and mummy had already been stolen. Then they would leave, not realizing that Khufu's real burial chamber was still hidden somewhere else inside the pyramid.

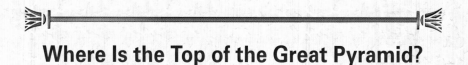

Where Is the Top of the Great Pyramid?

Egyptologists think that when the Great Pyramid was first built, it was topped with a pyramidion, or miniature pyramid. The stone pyramidion was about 4 feet (1.2 m) high and may have been covered with gold. What happened to the pyramidion? Did ancient robbers steal it so the gold could be melted down? Or is the lost golden tip of the pyramid buried or hidden somewhere, still to be discovered?

This is the pyramidion from one of Pharaoh Sneferu's pyramids.

Glossary

afterlife (AF-tur-*life*) the life a person has after he or she dies

amputated (AM-pyoo-*tay*-tid) cut off for medical reasons, usually an arm or leg

archaeologists (*ar*-kee-OL-uh-jists) scientists who learn about ancient times by studying things they dig up, such as tombs and tools

astronomers (uh-STRAHN-uh-murz) scientists who study planets, stars, and space

caliph (KAL-if) a Muslim ruler and religious leader from history

cemetery (SEM-uh-*terr*-ee) an area of land where dead bodies are buried

chanting (CHANT-ing) singing or shouting in a repetitive, rhythmic way; workers might chant as a way to encourage each other and work in unison

Egyptologists (ee-jip-TAHL-uh-jists) historians or scientists who study ancient Egypt

elaborate (ih-LA-buh-ruht) detailed or highly decorated

embalmers (em-BALM-urz) people who prepare dead bodies for burial

evidence (EV-uh-duhnss) objects or information used to prove something

hieroglyphs (HYE-ur-uh-*glifss*) pictures used in ancient Egyptian writing

intriguing (in-TREEG-ing) fascinating

manual (MAN-yoo-uhl) physical work that is done by a person without using machines

mourners (MORN-urz) people who grieve for a dead person and attend his or her funeral

pharaoh (FAIR-oh) a ruler of ancient Egypt

preserved (prih-ZURVD) treated something to stop it from rotting

pyramid (PEER-uh-mid) a stone building with a square base and triangular sides that meet at a point on top

quarry (KWOR-ee) an open pit from which stone or other material is dug up

sarcophagus (sar-KAHF-uh-guhss) a stone box made for holding a coffin

spirits (SPIHR-its) the parts of people that may go on after death

stonemasons (STOHN-may-suhnz) people who carve statues or build structures from stone

symbolic (sim-BAHL-ik) standing for, or representing, something else

temples (TEM-puhlz) religious buildings where people worship

theory (THIHR-ee) an idea, based on limited information, that explains certain facts or events

vizier (vih-ZEER) an important official who may design tombs and other structures, and then manage the construction process

Bibliography

www.aeraweb.org/sphinx-project/

Romer, John. *The Great Pyramid: Ancient Egypt Revisited.* Cambridge, UK: Cambridge University Press (2007).

Read More

Chrisp, Peter. *Pyramid (DK: Experience).* New York: Dorling Kindersley (2006).

Leardi, Jeanette. *The Great Pyramid: Egypt's Tomb for All Time (Castles, Palaces & Tombs).* New York: Bearport (2007).

Morley, Jacqueline. *You Wouldn't Want to Be a Pyramid Builder!: A Hazardous Job You'd Rather Not Have.* New York: Franklin Watts (2014).

Stanborough, Rebecca. *The Great Pyramid of Giza (Fact Finders: Engineering Wonders).* North Mankato, MN: Capstone (2016).

Learn More Online

To learn more about the Great Pyramid, visit
www.bearportpublishing.com/EgyptsAncientSecrets

Index

About the Author

Ruth Owen has written many nonfiction books for children.
She has always been fascinated by ancient Egyptian history
and the work of archaeologists.